LIGHTHOUSES OF MAINE

*T*his pictorial guide leads you from south to north along the beautiful Maine Coast. We start at Whaleback Light, on the Maine-New Hampshire border and finish with Whitlocks Mill Light, on the St. Croix River near Calais and bordering New Brunswick.

*S*ixty-six lighthouses dot Maine's vast coastline. Many of the lighthouses on the mainland can be reached with comparative ease. The offshore lighthouses are accessible only with special transportation; i.e. by ferry, scheduled or chartered boat, plane or a friendly lobsterman. Three of the lighthouses pictured are in Canada, however, most easily visited from Maine. Mulholland Light and East Quoddy Head Light are on Campobello Island, near Lubec and Machias Seal Island is 12 miles off the Maine Coast near Cutler.

A visit to the museums in Maine that feature lighthouses would provide additional information. Several are: The Museum at Portland Head Light in Cape Elizabeth, Portland Harbor Museum in So. Portland, Maine Maritime Museum in Bath, Marshall Point Lighthouse Museum in Port Clyde, Shore Village Museum also known as Maine's Lighthouse Museum in Rockland, Fisherman's Museum at Pemaquid Point Lighthouse, Museum at Monhegan Island Light and the Penobscot Marine Museum in Searsport.

*W*e hope you will enjoy our pictorial guide book and will have a chance to visit some of our lighthouses during your travels in Maine.

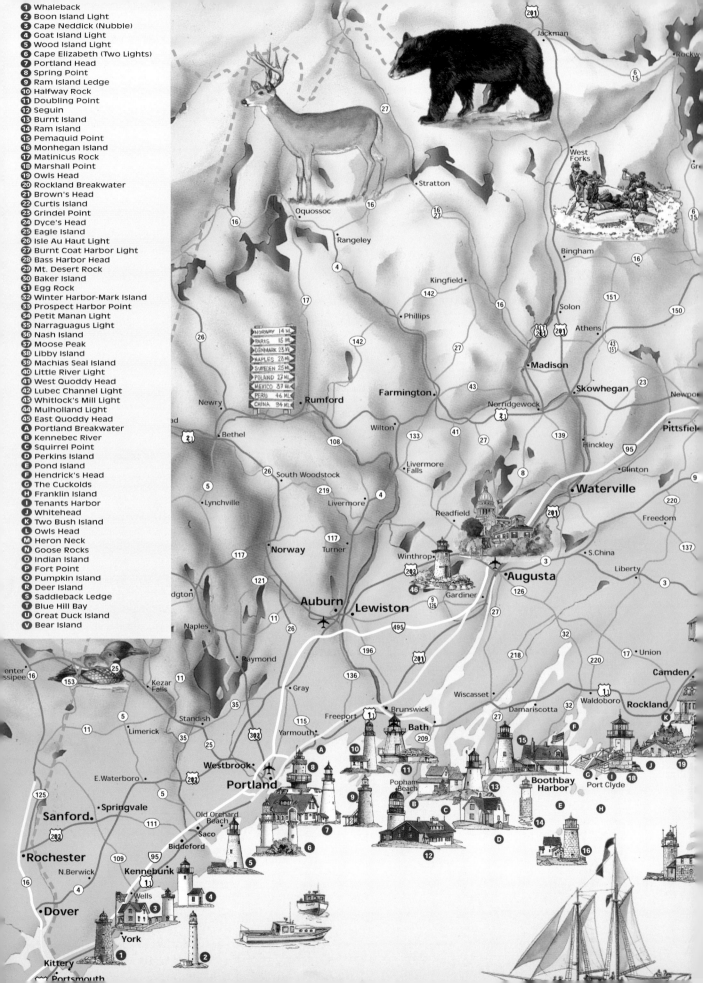

1. Whaleback
2. Boon Island Light
3. Cape Neddick (Nubble)
4. Goat Island Light
5. Wood Island Light
6. Cape Elizabeth (Two Lights)
7. Portland Head
8. Spring Point
9. Ram Island Ledge
10. Halfway Rock
11. Doubling Point
12. Seguin
13. Burnt Island
14. Ram Island
15. Pemaquid Point
16. Monhegan Island
17. Matinicus Rock
18. Marshall Point
19. Owls Head
20. Rockland Breakwater
21. Brown's Head
22. Curtis Island
23. Grindel Point
24. Dyce's Head
25. Eagle Island
26. Isle Au Haut Light
27. Burnt Coat Harbor Light
28. Bass Harbor Head
29. Mt. Desert Rock
30. Baker Island
31. Egg Rock
32. Winter Harbor-Mark Island
33. Prospect Harbor Point
34. Petit Manan Light
35. Narraguagus Light
36. Nash Island
37. Moose Peak
38. Libby Island
39. Machias Seal Island
40. Little River Light
41. West Quoddy Head
42. Lubec Channel Light
43. Whitlock's Mill Light
44. Mulholland Light
45. East Quoddy Head
A. Portland Breakwater
B. Kennebec River
C. Squirrel Point
D. Perkins Island
E. Pond Island
F. Hendrick's Head
G. The Cuckolds
H. Franklin Island
I. Tenants Harbor
J. Whitehead
K. Two Bush Island
L. Owls Head
M. Heron Neck
N. Goose Rocks
O. Indian Island
P. Fort Point
Q. Pumpkin Island
R. Deer Island
S. Saddleback Ledge
T. Blue Hill Bay
U. Great Duck Island
V. Bear Island

BAXTER
STATE
PARK

Houlton

Island Falls

Patten

11

2A

Millin ocket

Haynesville

Medway

1

157

Reed

95

Danforth

Mattawamkeag

Dover-
Foxcroft

Milo

Lincoln

6

Spingfield

Topsfield

West
Ehfield

6
16

6
155

Dexter

15

East
Corinth

Princeton

1

11
43

21

Calais

Baring

43

222

Old
Town

9

Orono

Wesley

191

Grove

45

Bangor

Amherst

Aurora

Beddington

192

Perry

202

Dixmont

E.Eddington

9

181

Dennysville

44

1A

46

1A

179

Waltham

193

Northfield

86

Eastport

Bucksport

Deblois

Whiting

Lubec

Stockton
Springs

175

Columbia
Falls

189

42

Belfast

P

1

Ellsworth

182

Cherryfield

Machias

East
Machias

191

41

23

172

3

1A

187

Cutler

24

Castine

Blue
Hill

Winter Harbor

32

Gouldsboro

35

Jonesport

38

40

O

102

31

Milbridge

36

37

39

22

ACADIA
NAT'L
PK.

V

34

20

N

125

28

33

Stonington

R

T

27

U

M

ACADIA
NAT'L
PK.

26

30

S

21

29

17

Whaleback Light

Built in 1820, Whaleback is located off the coast of Kittery Point, Maine, yet protects Portsmouth Harbor. Both Maine and New Hampshire like to lay claim to Whaleback but the lighthouse is positioned closer to Maine. The current 72 foot tall unpainted granite tower was constructed in 1872 and fitted with a fourth-order lens. The white flashing light and foghorn are both automated.

Boon Island Light

Established in 1811, the lighthouse stands on a small rocky island 6 1/2 miles off the coast southeast of Cape Neddick. This lighthouse is one of the most isolated along the coast and has been damaged numerous times by severe storms. The first 50 foot wooden tower was established in 1800. This tower was destroyed and replaced in 1804. A new light tower was authorized in 1812 but storms destroyed the light again in 1831. The current tower which stands 137 feet high is the tallest in New England. Its 70,000 candlepower light can be seen for 18 miles.

Cape Neddick Light

Also called "Nubble Light", built in 1879, it is the southernmost lighthouse in Maine. Situated on a barren rock island "the Nubble" off Cape Neddick, this lighthouse is considered one of the most popular scenic attractions along the coast.

The 41-foot cast iron tower is fitted with a fourth-order lens, flashing red every six seconds. Nubble's height above water is 88 feet with a range of 13 nautical miles.

Wood Island Light

The lighthouse marks the entrance of the Saco River and lies just offshore from Biddeford Pool. This lighthouse, built in 1808 and rebuilt in 1858, sits on the east end of Wood Island. The light was automated in 1986. Its height above water is 71 feet with a range of 24 nautical miles.

Goat Island Light

The lighthouse, built in 1822 and rebuilt in 1859, sits on the southwest end of Goat Island near the entrance to Cape Porpoise Harbor. This lighthouse was Maine's last manned light station, not automated until 1990. Its height above water is 38 feet with a range of 12 nautical miles.

Cape Elizabeth Light

Also called "Two Lights", built in 1828, they were located near Two Lights State Park. The west tower was dismanteled in 1824 and the keeper's house is now privately owned. The east tower, visible for 27 nautical miles, is the most powerful beacon on the New England coast, at four-million candle power. Two Lights height above water is 129 feet.

Portland Head Light

The oldest lighthouse in Maine, Portland Head Light has guided maritime traffic through the entrance to Portland Harbor for over 200 years. Local merchants began petitioning the Massachusetts legislature for a lighthouse at Portland Head as early as 1784. A maritime tragedy in 1787 finally prompted the legislature to approve a small appropriation of $750.00 to begin construction of a 58 foot tower of rubblestone set in lime.

The Lighthouse Act of 1789 transferred responsibility for aids to navigation from the individual states to the Federal Government and in 1790 under the authorization from President George Washingon, $1500.00 was appropriated for the completion of the lighthouse. Portland Head Light flickered into operation just before sunset on January 10, 1791. Portland Head Light is on the National Register of Historic Places.

Photo © Jim Abts

Spring Point Light

The lighthouse was originally built in 1855 and rebuilt prior to 1897. It is located offshore from Fort Preble, marking the west side of the main entrance to Portland Harbor. The present 40 foot caisson type concrete tower was built in 1897. First constructed as an offshore light, not until 1951 was it connected to the mainland by a 900-foot breakwater. The light was automated in 1934.

Portland Breakwater Light

Also called "Bug Light", it was built in 1855, replaced in 1875, automated in 1934 and is currently inactive. The lighthouse underwent major renovation in 1990 and is listed on the National Register of Historic Places. The lighthouse, complete with its Corinthian Columns, was created to resemble a 4th century Greek monument.

Ram Island Ledge Light

It was built in 1905 to ease the cause of many shipwrecks that ran upon the ledge at high tide. The lighthouse was constructed of gray granite blocks, cut and transported from Vinalhaven. The light was automated in 1959. Located offshore from Fort Williams Park, Cape Elizabeth, its height above water is 77 feet with a range of 12 nautical miles.

Halfway Rock Light

It derives its name from its location, sitting on a barren three acre rock ledge halfway between Cape Elizabeth and Cape Small in Casco Bay. Halfway Rock is located 11 miles northeast of Portland Head and protects this busy shipping lane. The 66 foot granite tower was completed in 1871 and fitted with a third-order Fresnel lens. The light was automated in 1975.

Doubling Point Light

Built in 1898, the lighthouse is located on Arrowsic Island. It aids mariners navigating the Kennebec River to the shipbuilding town of Bath.

Squirrel Point Light

Completed in 1898, it is located at the southwest tip of Arrowsic Island on the Kennebec River. The lighthouse is situated opposite Phippsburg village. The 25 foot tower was fitted with a fifth-order Fresnel lens. The light was automated in 1979.

Perkins Island Light

Built in 1898, it is one of four light-houses located on the Kennebec River. The lighthouse is situated on the east-side of the Kennebec near Parker Head.

Pond Island Light

Built in 1821 and rebuilt in 1855,it is located on a small island at the mouth of the Kennebec River near Popham Beach.

Kennebec River Light

Also called "Doubling Point Range Lights", built in 1908, located near Doubling Point Light, it has two towers positioned to assist in navigating the Kennebec River. The front range light is 21 feet high and the rear light is 13 feet tall. Both towers were originally fitted with a fifth-order Fresnel lens. The range lights were automated in 1990.

Seguin Island Light

The original 38 foot tower was built in 1875, by order of President George Washington at a cost of $ 6,300.00. Located two miles south of the mouth of the Kennebec River, Seguin Light was Maine's second lighthouse. The lighthouse has been rebuilt twice, in 1820 and 1857. The present tower, 57 feet tall and 186 feet above the water, is the highest above water on the Maine coast. It can be seen at a distance of 40 miles. The tower accomodates Maine's only first-order lens. The light also has one of the most powerful foghorns made. The light was automated in 1985 and the Coast Guard maintains it. The island and keepers quarters are maintained by the Friends of Seguin Island, a non-profit organization. A small museum is located on the north side of the keeper's house.

Hendrick's Head Light

Built in 1829, it is on Southport Island on the east side of the mouth of the Sheepscot River. The current 39 foot tall tower was built in 1875. The station, dicontinued in 1933 and automated in 1951, is now privately owned. The property has been carefully and accurately restored by the current owners.

Cuckolds Light

Established as a fog signal station in 1892, it had the light tower added in 1907. The light was automated in 1975. Cuckolds sits on a small island less than a mile from the tip of Southport Island and the village of Newagen. Its height above water is 59 feet with a range of 12 nautical miles.

Burnt Island Light

It was built in 1821 and altered in 1888. Changes were made because its light interfered with the light from Cuckolds Light. Burnt Island Light is located on the west side entrance to Boothbay Harbor. Its height above water is 61 feet. The red and white light flashes with a range of red, 12 nautical miles and white, 15 nautical miles.

Ram Island Light

Built in 1883, this lighthouse is located on Ram Island off Ocean Point. It guards the channel "Fisherman's Passage". The light was automated in 1965 and after falling into disrepair, was rebuilt by the Coast Guard in 1977.

Pemaquid Point Light

Comissioned in 1827 by John Quincy Adams, it is located on the west side of the entrance to Muscongus Bay, in New Harbor. The lighthouse was rebuilt in 1857 and automated in 1934. The keeper's house is home for the "Fisherman's Museum", operated by the town of Bristol. Its height above water is 79 feet, with a range of 14 nautical miles.

Monhegan Island Light

Franklin Island Light

The lighthouse is on Franklin Island in Muscongus Bay five miles offshore from Friendship. Built in 1803, under the order of President Thomas Jefferson, this is Maine's third oldest lighthouse.

The lighthouse is located at the center of the island at the island's highest elevation. At 178 feet above the water, it is the second highest along the Maine coast. The lighthouse was built in 1824 and rebuilt in 1850. Its flashing white light has a range of 21 nautical miles and was automated in 1959. The keeper's house is now a museum. Monhegan Island is 10 miles off the Maine coast, south of Port Clyde. Settled in 1614, the island represents Maine's earliest fishing village.

Photo © Marjorie Monteleon

Matinicus Rock Light

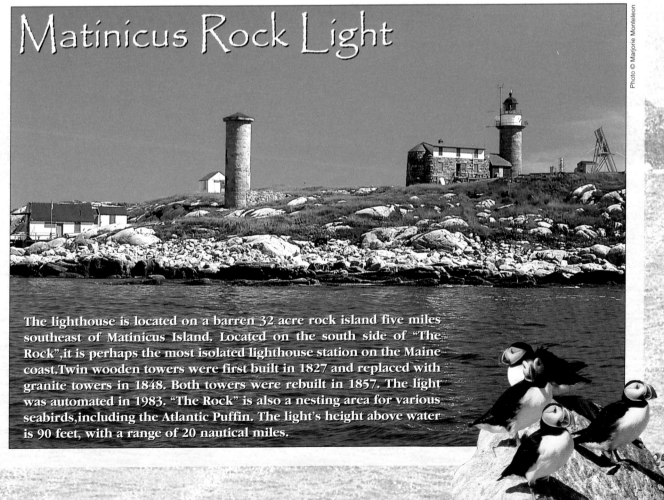

The lighthouse is located on a barren 32 acre rock island five miles southeast of Matinicus Island. Located on the south side of "The Rock", it is perhaps the most isolated lighthouse station on the Maine coast. Twin wooden towers were first built in 1827 and replaced with granite towers in 1848. Both towers were rebuilt in 1857. The light was automated in 1983. "The Rock" is also a nesting area for various seabirds, including the Atlantic Puffin. The light's height above water is 90 feet, with a range of 20 nautical miles.

Marshall Point Light

Built in 1832 and rebuilt in 1857, the lighthouse marks the eastern boundary of Muscongus Bay and the entrance to Port Clyde Harbor. The light was automated in 1980 and the town of St. George acquired the keeper's house and grounds. The keeper's house was placed on the National Register of Historic Places in 1988. Restored by the St. George Historical Society, the keeper's house is now home for the Marshall Point Lighthouse Museum. The light's height above water is 30 feet, with a range of 13 nautical miles.

Tenants Harbor Light

This lighthouse, located at the east end of the 22 acre Southern Island, aided mariners navigating Penobscot Bay and entering Tenants Harbor. The 27 foot brick tower was built in 1857 and fitted with a fourth-order Fresnel lens. The lighthouse was discontinued in 1934 and the property auctioned, later owned by artist Andrew Wyeth. The property is now owned by his son, Jamie Wyeth. The pyramidam bell tower serves as his studio.

Whitehead Light

It was constructed under the order of Thomas Jefferson in 1807, making this one of Maine's oldest lighthouses. Located on a small island off Tenants Harbor, this lighthouse marks the western entrance to Muscle Ridge Channel. The original light and keeper's house were stone structures. In 1852, a new 41 foot granite tower was added along with a new wooden keeper's house. A third-order Fresnel lens was added in 1857. Whitehead was Maine's first lightstation to have a one-room schoolhouse. The light was automated in 1982.

Two Bush Island Light

Photo © Marjorie Monteleon

The lighthouse takes its name from two lone pine trees that served as day beacons before the 42-foot square lighthouse was built in 1897. Located just outside Penobscot Bay, it guards the north end entrance of Two Bush Channel and the east side entrance to Muscle Ridge Channel. The light was automated in 1964.

Owl's Head Light

Photo © Jim Abts

Built in 1825, it guards the south entrance to Rockland Harbor. The lighthouse, only 20 feet tall, stands 100 feet above the water. Owl's Head Light is on the National Register of Historic Places. The light has a range of 16 nautical miles.

Rockland Breakwater Light

Built in 1888, it is at the end of the mile long stone breakwater extending into Rockland Harbor from Jameson Point. Construction of the breakwater started in 1881 and was completed in 1889. The present lighthouse was constructed in 1902 and automated in 1964. The light's height above water is 39 feet, with a range of 17 nautical miles.

Brown's Head Light

Photo © David Ransaw

The lighthouse was originally built in 1832 and rebuilt in 1857. It is located on the northeast point of Vinalhaven Island, the entrance to Fox Island Thorofare. The fog bell tower was removed after automation in 1987. Brown's Head height above water is 39 feet.

Heron Neck Light

Photo © Jim Abts

The light is located on the southern tip of Green Island, just south of Carver's Harbor on Vinalhaven Island. Heron Neck was built in 1854 and guards the east entrance to Hurricane Sound. A fire nearly destroyed the keeper's house in 1989; however the property has been completely restored.

Goose Rocks Light

Photo © Jim Abts

Built in 1890, it sits on a ledge marking the east entrance to Fox Island Thorofare. The lighthouse guards the busy waterway between Vinalhaven and North Haven islands. The structure is a typical caisson-type or "spark-plug" style. This 51 foot tower, originally fitted with a fourth-order lens, is now solar powered.

Indian Island Light

First established in 1850, the lighthouse was a lantern mounted on the keeper's house. It was discontinued for a short time after 1856 and reactivated with a new lighthouse tower in 1875. The lighthouse was discontinued in 1934 and is now privately owned.

Curtis Island Light

Built in 1836 and re-built in 1896, it is on the south side entrance to Camden Harbor. This five acre island is named after Cyris Curtis, founder of the Saturday Evening Post. This lighthouse has a fixed beacon which is 52 feet above water, with a range of 6 nautical miles. The light was automated in 1972 and deeded to the town of Camden.

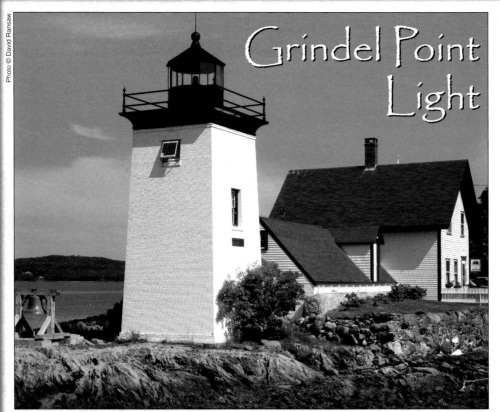

Photo © David Ransaw

Grindel Point Light

Built in 1851, it guards the north side entrance to Gilkey Harbor on Islesboro Island. The present square brick tower was constructed in 1874. The lighthouse was deactivated in 1934 and given to the town of Islesboro. The lighthouse was recommissioned in 1987 and is now solar powered. The Islesboro Sailors Memorial Museum is located in the keeper's house. The fog bell on the southside of the light tower is on loan from the Shore Village Museum in Rockland, Maine. The light's height above water is 39 feet, with a range of 6 nautical miles.

Fort Point Light

Photo © Kevin Shields

Built in 1836 and rebuilt in 1857, it is located on the west-side mouth of the Penobscot River in Cape Jellison near Searsport. Its 31 foot square brick tower still stands today. In 1890 a bell tower was added and is currently listed on the National Register of Historic Places. The light was automated in 1988.

Dyce's Head Light

The light was constructed in 1829 and remodeled in 1858. The keeper's house was again rebuilt in 1937. The entire property is owned and maintained by the town of Castine. The light guards the north side entrance to Castine Harbor. Castine, because of its strategic location, has been occupied by the British, French, and Dutch, thus having flown the flags of four nations. The keeper's house was recently destroyed by fire but it has been restored.

Pumpkin Island Light

Established in 1854, it marks the western entrance to Eggemoggin Reach on Little Deer Isle. The light was automated in 1930 and is now privately owned.

Eagle Island Light

Built in 1839 and rebuilt in 1858, it sits on a bluff at the northeast end of Eagle Island. This 260 acre island lies halfway between Deer Isle and North Haven. The light was automated in 1959. In 1963 the keeper's house was burned and other structures on the property demolished but the lighthouse and bell tower were saved. It is now being restored. Its height above water is 106 feet, with a range of 9 nautical miles.

Deer Island Thorofare Light

Saddleback Ledge Light

Photo © Marjorie Monteleon

Photo © Marjorie Monteleon

Also called "Mark Island Light" it was built in 1857. The lighthouse is on the west side of Mark Island and guards the western entrance of the thorofare. The 25 foot tower was first fitted with a fourth-order Fresnel lens. Automated in 1958, the lens was replaced with a modern optic.

It sits on a rock ledge between Vinalhaven and Isle au Haut, at the southern end of Isle au Haut Bay. The lighthouse was established in 1839 and the rugged 42 foot granite tower still stands. The light was automated in 1954.

Blue Hill Bay Light

Photo © Courtney Thompson

Located on Green Island, one of the four islands called Fly Islands. Established in 1857, this lighthouse on the western edge of Blue Hill Bay guides mariners into Eggemoggin Reach. The lighthouse was discontinued in 1933 and automated in 1935. The property, now privately owned, has been carefully restored.

Isle au Haut Light

Isle au Haut, named high island by French explorer Samuel de Champlain in 1604, is located six miles south of Stonington. The island is part of Acadia National Park. The lighthouse, located on Robinson Point, was built in 1907 and automated in 1934. The property (except the tower) was sold at an auction. The tower is still maintained by the Coast Guard. The keeper's house, now operated as a bed and breakfast, is on the National Register of Historic Places.

Bass Harbor Light

The lighthouse is located on the southwest point of Mt. Desert Island, marking the entrance to Blue Hill Bay and Bass Harbor. The lighthouse was built in 1858 to assist ships seeking shelter in the harbor. The 32 foot tall brick tower is now automated, with an occulating red light. Its height above water is 56 feet, with a range of 13 nautical miles.

Mount Desert Rock Light

Established in 1830, the lighthouse is one of the most isolated on the Maine coast. It marks the entrance to Frenchman and Blue Hill Bays. The island is located some 25 nautical miles south of Mount Desert Island. In 1857, a 58 foot granite tower replaced the original wooden structure. The property is currently leased by the College of the Atlantic for use as a whale watching station.

Burnt Coat Harbor Light

Also called "Hockamock Head", it was originally built in 1872 on the southwest tip of Swans Island guarding the entrance to Burnt Coat Harbor. The original fourth-order lens was removed in 1975 when the light was automated.

Great Duck Island Light

Established in 1890, it sits on the south end of the island. Great Duck Island is located about 5 1/2 miles southeast of Bass Harbor. The 42 foot granite tower was originally fitted with a fifth-order Fresnel lens. The light was automated in 1986 and is now owned by the Maine Chapter of Nature Conservancy

Baker Island Light

Egg Rock Light

The lighthouse was established in 1828, marking the southeast entrance to Frenchman's Bay. The present 43 foot brick tower was built in 1855 and fitted with a fourth-order Fresnel lens. The light was automated and converted to solar power in 1966. Baker Island is part of Acadia National Park.

Built in 1875, it sits on a rocky ledge marking the entrance to Frenchman's Bay. The light was automated in 1976. Many sightseeing and whale watching boats from Bar Harbor pass by this lighthouse.

Bear Island Light

It was established in 1839 under the order of President Martin Van Buren. Bear Island is one of the five islands that are called the Cranberry Islands. The lighthouse aids mariners at the southeast entrance to Northeast Harbor. The current 31 foot brick tower was constructed in 1889. Its light flashes white at 100 feet above the water. The property is now part of Acadia National Park.

Mark Island Light

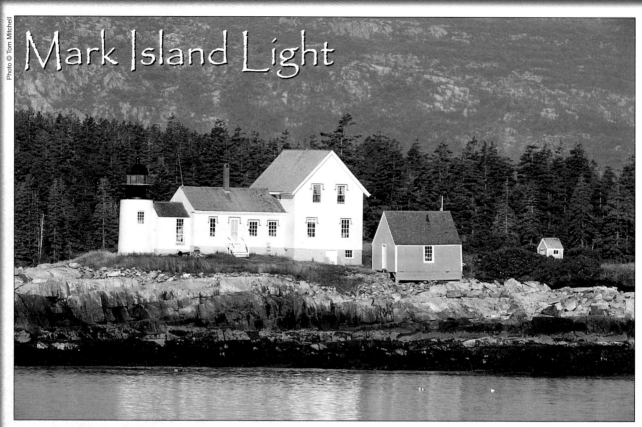

Also called "Winter Harbor Light", the lighthouse was established in 1856 and now privately owned, It is situated on Mark Island in Frenchman's Bay, across from Bar Harbor.

Narraguagus Light

Also called "Pond Island Light", established in 1856, the lighthouse is located on Pond Island in Narraguagus Bay, south of Milbridge. The lighthouse was authorized to mark the entrance to Milbridge Harbor. The lighthouse was discontinued in 1934 and is now privately owned.

Petit Manan Light

Established in 1817 and rebuilt with granite in 1855, Petit Manan is the second tallest lighthouse in Maine. The current tower stands 119 feet tall and is located on the east point of Petit Manan Island, 2 1/2 miles off Petit Manan Point in South Milbridge. The station also is equipped with a fog signal. This location is engulfed in fog nearly 20% of the time. Its height is 123 feet above the water, with a range of 26 nautical miles.

Prospect Harbor Light

This lighthouse, built in 1850 and rebuilt in 1891, marks the east side entrance to the inner harbor. The property is now part of an active military base. The light was automated in 1934.

Nash Island Light

Built in 1838, this lighthouse marks the entrance to Moose-A-Bec Reach, Pleasant Bay and Harrington Bay near South Addison. The original tower was rebuilt in 1873 and the 51 foot square brick tower still stands today. The light was automated in 1958 and discontinued in 1982.

Moose Peak Light

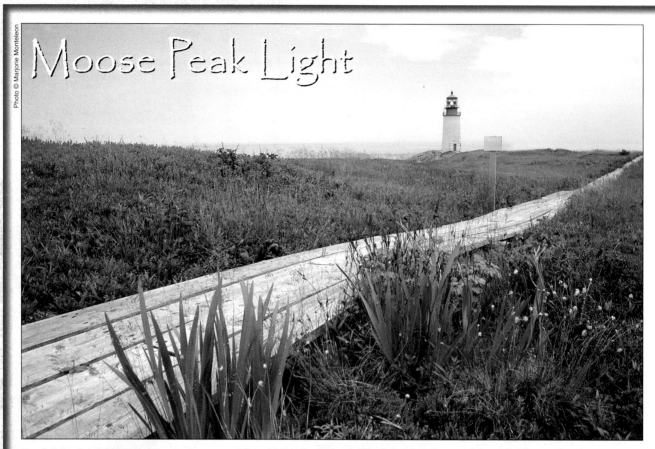

Photo © Marjorie Monteleon

Established in 1827, it sits on the east side of Mistake Island. The island is located five miles south of Jonesport. Moose Peak Light was recorded to be the foggiest light station on the Maine coast. It was automated in 1972.

Libby Island Light

Photo © Courtney Thompson

Marking the east entrance to Machias Bay, it was commonly known as Machias Light. The present 42 foot granite tower was built in 1824 on the southern tip of Libby Island. The island is actually two islands connected by a sandbar. The light was automated in 1974.

Little River Light

It was built in 1847 on Little River Island at the entrance to Cutler Harbor. The current 41 foot cast iron tower was built in 1876. The keeper's house was replaced in 1888. Little River Light was automated in 1975.

Machias Seal Island Light

Located 12 miles off the coast near Cutler, the island is a noted breeding ground and haven for the Atlantic Sea Puffin. Owned by the United States, the island and lighthouse are operated by the Canadian goverment.

West Quoddy Light

Located on the easternmost point of the continental United States, this red and white striped lighthouse marks the southwest entrance to Quoddy Channel.

The lighthouse was originally built in 1807 under the orders of Thomas Jefferson, then rebuilt in 1858. The light's height above water is 83 feet, with a range of 18 nautical miles.

Lubec Channel Light

It was built in 1889, marking the western entrance to Lubec Harbor. The lighthouse is the "sparkplug" cast-iron style. It was fitted with a fifth-order Fresnel lens. The lighthouse was due to be discontinued in 1989. Local residents rallied behind a "Save The Sparkplug" compaign and in 1992 Lubec Channel Light was restored.

Whitlocks Mill Light

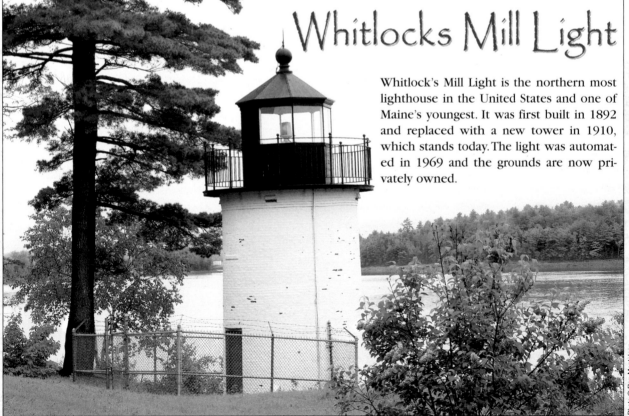

Whitlock's Mill Light is the northern most lighthouse in the United States and one of Maine's youngest. It was first built in 1892 and replaced with a new tower in 1910, which stands today. The light was automated in 1969 and the grounds are now privately owned.

Mulholland Light

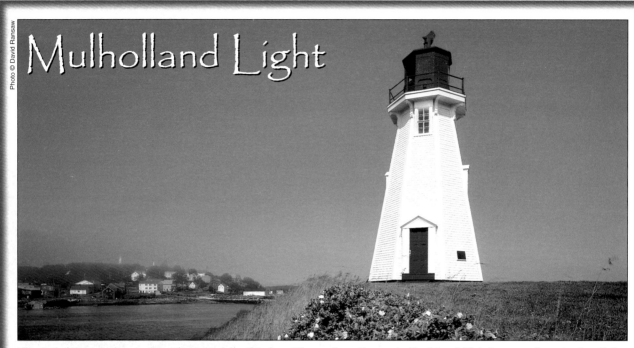

The lighthouse is located on the east side of Lubec Channel on Campobello Island. This is a non-functioning light.

East Quoddy Light

Also called "Head Harbor Light", it is located on the northern end of Campobello Island, New Brunswick. The lighthouse is maintained by the Canadian Coast Guard. The large red and white cross, typical of Canadian lighthouses, is intended to make visibilty against a snowy background.